Wealthy Living

Overcoming Personal Finance Obstacles

Table of Contents

1. Introduction 1

2. Building the Foundation: Basics of Personal Finance 2

    2.1. Understanding Personal Finance 2

    2.2. Financial Planning: Where it All Begins 2

    2.3. Income: The Linchpin 3

    2.4. Budgeting: Your Financial Blueprint 3

    2.5. The Role of Savings 3

    2.6. Debt Management 4

    2.7. Investing for Growth 4

    2.8. Retirement Planning 4

    2.9. Insurance: Your Financial Shield 4

    2.10. Estate Planning 5

3. Unmasking the Common: Personal Finance Myths 6

    3.1. Myth One: More Money Means Fewer Problems 6

    3.2. Myth Two: Debt Is Always Bad 7

    3.3. Myth Three: All Investments Are High Risk 7

    3.4. Myth Four: Only High Earners Can Save 7

    3.5. Myth Five: I'm Too Young To Start Planning For Retirement . . 8

4. Breaking the Chains: Eliminating Debts Effectively 9

    4.1. Before You Begin The Debt Elimination Journey 9

    4.2. Creating a Budget 9

    4.3. Debt Payment Strategy 10

    4.4. Negotiation with Creditors 10

    4.5. Balance Transfers 10

    4.6. Debt Consolidation 11

    4.7. Seeking Professional Help 11

5. Mastering the Game: Understanding Financial Markets 12

    5.1. Understanding the Basics: The Financial Market 12

5.2. The Different Types of Financial Markets 13

5.3. How to Navigate through Financial Markets 14

6. Invest to Impress: Strategies for Profitable Investing 16

6.1. Understanding Investment Basics 16

6.2. The Time Value of Money 16

6.3. Investing in Stocks 17

6.4. Bond Investments 17

6.5. Real Estate and Commodities 18

6.6. Planning for Retirement 18

6.7. Embracing Robo-Advisors 18

7. Cultivating Prosperity: Smart Savings Techniques 20

7.1. The Frugal Fortress: Enlist Your Expenses 20

7.2. A Dose of Preventive Healthcare: Insurance Savings 21

7.3. Automate Your Savings Journey 21

7.4. Investment: The Secret Armory 21

7.5. Retirement Planning: A Future-Proof Life 22

8. Shopping Smarter: Conscious Spending Tactics 23

8.1. Considering Needs Vs Wants 23

8.2. Creating and Sticking to a Budget 23

8.3. Understanding the True Cost of a Purchase 24

8.4. Comparing to Conserve 24

8.5. Practicing Mindful Spending 24

8.6. Buying Quality Products 25

8.7. Avoiding Debt Traps 25

9. Ready for Rainy Days: An Insight into Emergency Funds 26

9.1. Understanding the Emergency Fund 26

9.2. Building Your Emergency Fund 27

9.3. Making the Best Use of your Fund 28

9.4. Grow your Emergency Fund: A Final Word 28

10. Planning for a Worry-Free Future: Retirement Strategies 30

10.1. Understanding Your Financial Situation 30

10.2. Determining Retirement Goals 31

10.3. Creating a Saving and Investment Plan 31

10.4. Insurance Coverage in Retirement 32

11. Your Wealth, Your Legacy: Estate Planning Essentials 33

11.1. The Basics of Estate Planning 33

11.2. Wills and Trusts in Estate Planning 34

11.3. Estate Taxes and Legalities 34

11.4. Estate planning and Retirement Funds 35

11.5. Choosing the Correct Executor and Legal Counsel 35

11.6. All About Updating Your Estate Plan 35

11.7. Concluding Thoughts 36

Chapter 1. Introduction

Unveil the golden keys to Prosperity Palace as we journey together in our Special Report: "Wealthy Living: Overcoming Personal Finance Obstacles". In a world where the whispers of fiscal difficulties can often drown out the echoes of success, we have carved a beacon of hope, an opportunity for you to rise above the turbulent sea of financial uncertainties. This report is not a treasure map filled with complex jargons, but rather your compass, a cheerful guide through easy-to-understand strategies and practical advice. Unravel the secret codes to healthy money management, conscientious spending, optimal saving, and profitable investing, all designed to escalate you to a life of luxury and financial freedom. Let this be your call to action, to pivot from existing challenges to flourishing opportunities, and embrace the wealthy living you so rightfully deserve! Jump in, for a wonderful journey awaits. Get ready to buy your ticket to financial success with our Special Report!

Chapter 2. Building the Foundation: Basics of Personal Finance

In the pursuit of financial acumen and fiscal independence, understanding the basics of personal finance lays the groundwork. Though it might appear complex at the outset, grasping these fundamentals empowers you to take control of your financial future. Let's gradually peel back the layers of this complex world.

2.1. Understanding Personal Finance

Personal finance refers to the broad management of individual or a family's financial activities. This includes budgeting, income generation, investing, savings, insurance, and retirement planning. Its primary goal is to help you make the most of your financial resources and safeguard your financial health over the long-term.

2.2. Financial Planning: Where it All Begins

Financial planning is the starting point in your personal finance journey. This means identifying your financial goals both short-term, such as saving for a vacation, and long-term, such as planning for retirement. Once these are defined, tailor your financial plan to help achieve these goals and track your progress.

2.3. Income: The Linchpin

It's impossible to discuss personal finance without mentioning income, as it's the fuel that drives your financial engine. Your income may come from multiple sources: full-time work, part-time jobs, passive income, inheritance, etc. The key is to understand the components of your income and leverage it effectively in achieving your financial aspirations.

2.4. Budgeting: Your Financial Blueprint

Budgeting is a crucial factor in personal finance, often likened to a roadmap or blueprint. Creating a budget involves following a set of steps:

1. Calculate your total income.

2. Enumerate your fixed and variable expenses.

3. Differentiate between needs and wants.

4. Set aside funds for savings and investments.

5. Analyze and adjust.

A well-planned budget will aid in managing your finances by allocating resources wisely and limiting overspending.

2.5. The Role of Savings

Think of savings as your financial safety net and as an enabler for future opportunities. A part of your monthly income should go towards savings, ideally at least 20%. This split is popularly known as the 50/30/20 rule where 50% goes towards needs, 30% towards wants, and 20% towards savings.

2.6. Debt Management

Debt, if not managed wisely, can quickly escalate and become an impediment to your financial freedom. Know the difference between good debt (like a home loan) and bad debt (like a high-interest credit card) and manage both effectively. Aim to eliminate bad debts at the earliest and make prudent use of good debts.

2.7. Investing for Growth

Investing your money wisely in various financial instruments can significantly augment your wealth. Before you plunge into investing, make sure you understand the associated risks and rewards. Not all investments are equal; some provide high returns but carry high risks, while others are low-risk but yield smaller returns. Therefore, diversification is key to balance risk and reward.

2.8. Retirement Planning

Ensuring a financially secured retirement requires meticulous planning and disciplined savings. Factors to consider include your targeted retirement age, possible medical costs, living expenses, etc. Generally, the earlier you start your retirement planning, the lesser the burden and the larger the corpus.

2.9. Insurance: Your Financial Shield

Insurance protects you from unforeseen financial losses. Various types of insurances (like health, life, auto, and home) protect different aspects of your life. It's important to evaluate and opt for insurance policies that cater to your specific needs.

2.10. Estate Planning

Estate planning, though often overlooked, is an integral part of personal finance. It ensures that in the event of your passing, your assets are distributed according to your wishes.

Dealing with personal finance often feels like a precarious balancing act, but with the right tools and proper knowledge, it will feel less like a high-wire act and more like a fun, empowering endeavor. Becoming financially literate doesn't happen overnight, but the importance of understanding these fundamentals can't be overstated. These foundational principles will empower you to navigate through your financial life, turning what once seemed like an intimidating maze into a well-tread path towards financial success.

Chapter 3. Unmasking the Common: Personal Finance Myths

Money myths, as many of us know, can somewhat be seductive. They promise quick fixes to touch problems, shortcuts to long processes, or counterintuitive insights that can magically swing your personal fortune in a new, lucrative direction.

However, the beautiful facade of these myths often hides the ugly truth: they can lead you away from practical, proven strategies and towards financial pitfalls. Bearing this in mind, we begin by identifying and debunking these commonly-held financial misconceptions.

3.1. Myth One: More Money Means Fewer Problems

While the allure of higher income is undeniable, more money does not necessarily equate to fewer problems. Income hikes may lead to lifestyle inflation, assuming bigger expenses and, potentially, higher levels of stress. By giving in to the temptation of luxuries that were once out of reach, we inadvertently widen our pool of wants without addressing our needs.

The true solution to this problem lies not in earning more but rather in mastering the art of budgeting. Knowing how to allocate your earnings properly, regardless of the amount, is essential.

3.2. Myth Two: Debt Is Always Bad

Many deem debt the enemy when it comes to personal finance management. However, truth be told, not all debt is detrimental. Certain kinds of debt, such as student loans or mortgages, can, in fact, open doors to new opportunities and long-term benefits.

The key to managing debt lies in differentiating between 'bad' and 'good' debt and understanding when to leverage each type for your benefit. 'Bad' debt, which is normally associated with depreciating assets such as credit card debt, spirals one into a trap. On the other hand, 'good' debt, associated with appreciating assets like an investment property, can potentially offer good returns overtime.

3.3. Myth Three: All Investments Are High Risk

Investments are often seen as a gamble, where one can either hit the jackpot or lose everything. However, investments are more than a game of luck, they are a science that require an understanding of risk and return.

There are investments with varying degrees of risk, and the trick is in knowing your risk tolerance level and diversifying your investment portfolio to balance potential returns against possible losses. Knowledge is power when it comes to investing, so don't let the fear of risk hold you back.

3.4. Myth Four: Only High Earners Can Save

This is a myth that is paralyzing in its impact. The notion that you need to be a high earner to save and secure your financial future is nothing but a limiting belief.

Real wealth comes from the habit of regular saving and investing over time, regardless of how much you earn. The compound interest on your savings would build up over time, setting you on the path to financial success. The sooner you start, no matter how small, the better your financial future.

3.5. Myth Five: I'm Too Young To Start Planning For Retirement

The belief that retirement planning should be postponed until later years is a grave financial blunder. In reality, the best time to start planning for retirement is as early as possible.

Compound interest rewards early and regular contributions, meaning the earlier you invest, the more your investment will grow. So instead of waiting until your golden years are on the horizon to start saving, plan early for a worry-free, comfortable retirement.

With these commonly-held financial myths unmasked, it's clear that personal finance management is as much about fact-checking and dispelling myths as it is about clever budgeting and investing. Analyze your personal finance practices against these debunked myths, and let the clarification guide your next steps towards financial freedom. Remember, it's not about making enormous leaps; rather, it's the culmination of small, consistent steps that lead to a life of financial wellness.

Chapter 4. Breaking the Chains: Eliminating Debts Effectively

Debt has often been referred to as the 'cement shoes' of personal finance. It pulls you down and prevents you from reaching your full economic potential. This chapter aims at providing you with time-tested strategies to get rid of this burden, eliminate your debts and set forth on the path to financial prosperity.

4.1. Before You Begin The Debt Elimination Journey

Understanding your current financial picture is the first step in resolving your debts. Generate a list of your monthly income sources and expenses. Create an exhaustive list of all your existing debts — from credit cards to mortgages, from personal loans to auto finance. Identify the balances, minimum payments, interest rates and monthly deadlines.

For debts, start from the one with the highest interest rate; this is your primary target. From there, arrange them in descending order of interest rates. This strategy, often known as the 'avalanche method,' will save you more money in the long run.

4.2. Creating a Budget

A successful debt elimination journey necessitates the creation of a stringent but realistic budget. It's about understanding your income and conversely, your spending habits. Allocate your monthly income toward fixed expenses, saving goals, and debt payments.

Remember, this budget is not designed to restrict you but to emphasize your financial situation. This perception change alone can motivate you toward your goals. Update this budget as necessary, keeping track of your payments and any changes to your income or expenses.

4.3. Debt Payment Strategy

Now, with a clearly defined budget and debt arrangement, structure your debt payment strategy. Pay the minimum on all of your debts each month, excluding the debt with the highest interest rate. Allocate the maximum of your resources to paying off this debt. Once this debt is paid off, move on to the next highest interest debt, so on and so forth. This continuation of the avalanche method gains momentum with every debt paid off and is compelling in reducing your overall liabilities.

In cases where morale is a potent factor, you may wish to consider the 'snowball method,' in which you start by paying off the debts with the smallest balance first, regardless of the interest rate.

4.4. Negotiation with Creditors

This subchapter aims to canvass the power of negotiation with your creditors. In some cases, speaking directly with your creditors can result in lowered interest rates or elimination of late fees. Always be prepared before such a call. Understand your situations, your ability to repay, and have a concise, clear proposal to put forth.

4.5. Balance Transfers

Balance transfers can be a powerful tool in tackling high-interest debts. This involves transferring your debt from a card account with a higher interest rate to one with a promotional lower or 0% rate.

This strategy is only effective if you have a clear plan to pay off the balance before the promotional rate ends.

4.6. Debt Consolidation

Debt consolidation merges multiple debts into one single loan with a lower interest rate, making payments more manageable. It's important to understand the terms of your new loan and ensure that the consolidation actually results in savings. This strategy can also have a positive impact on your credit score.

4.7. Seeking Professional Help

If your debts seem insurmountable, don't be afraid to seek professional help. Credit counselling agencies can provide guidance and may even negotiate with creditors on your behalf. While there's a nominal fee for these services, the benefits often far outweigh the costs.

Remember, the intention here isn't just to help eliminate your debts, but to teach you the strategies and tools necessary to remain debt-free. Like any journey, this will take time. Money habits, once ingrained, can be tough to change. But by creating a budget, exploring available tools, and remaining dedicated, you can eradicate your debts, break the chains of financial bondage, and set forth on a path to extensive economic prosperity - not just to survive, but to thrive.

Chapter 5. Mastering the Game: Understanding Financial Markets

Whether looking to elevate your existing wealth, or building your initial assets, it is indispensable to comprehend the underlying principles of global finance and the dynamism of the financial markets that dictate the ebbs and flows. It is significant to remember that the secret to prosperous living isn't just about accumulating wealth, but judiciously managing and multiplying it.

5.1. Understanding the Basics: The Financial Market

The financial market refers to the vast global network where buyers and sellers trade assets, including equities, bonds, currencies, derivatives, and commodities. Financial markets are vital for the overall economic health as they efficiently allocate global resources - they curate the perfect platform for businesses to raise capital, governments to finance public services, and investors to reach their financial goals.

To paint a clearer picture, imagine a bustling marketplace. This physical place of exchange is paralleled by the financial markets in the abstract sphere, where money is the commodity that gets exchanged for various other forms of capital. Yet, unlike a regular marketplace, the financial markets are significantly influenced by global events, regulations, economics, politics, and investor perceptions.

There are primarily two types of financial markets:

Primary markets: Where new stock and bond issues are sold to investors.

Secondary markets: Where existing securities are bought and sold.

5.2. The Different Types of Financial Markets

Financial markets can be further classified based on the types of securities they trade, their structure, the types of participants, and the conditions under which trades occur.

1. Capital markets: These include the stock and bond markets. Capital markets are vital for building wealth as they are where businesses go to raise cash to finance their operations and growth.

2. Money markets: Short-term debt instruments like Treasury bills, commercial paper, and certificates of deposit are traded in the money markets.

3. Foreign Exchange (Forex) markets: Forex markets are where currencies are traded. It's particularly crucial for businesses involved in international trade as well as for investors and traders who speculate on currencies' value.

4. Commodity markets: These markets trade in primary rather than manufactured products. Common examples are gold, cattle, wheat, and oil markets.

5. Derivatives markets: These markets trade in derivatives—financial instruments whose prices are derived from the price of something else. Derivatives' values are based on price movements in underlying assets, which range from commodities to currencies to stocks and market indexes.

===The Role of Financial Markets in Wealth Creation

Financial markets serve primarily six functions, all contributing to increased efficiency, wealth creation and economic growth:

1. Facilitating the exchange of funds Financial markets act as an intermediary for parties who have excess funds and those who require funds.

2. Determining price By matching supply and demand, financial markets establish the prices of various securities, which are indicative of their intrinsic value.

3. Liquidity Financial markets provide the convenience for parties to convert their assets into cash quickly and easily, thus imparting liquidity.

4. Risk Sharing By allowing asset price diversification, and through derivatives, they provide an avenue for risk sharing and hedging.

5. Collection and exchange of information Financial markets are an hub where vast amounts of information are collected, processed, and spread. This function is crucial for market transparency and efficiency.

6. Cost reduction Financial markets help in reducing transaction and information costs by providing valuable information and ensuring funds are channeled accurately.

5.3. How to Navigate through Financial Markets

Successfully threading through these markets involves more than just understanding the basics; it also necessitates strategic planning and well-informed decisions:

1. Study the market Stay updated with global and financial news. The effects of political, environmental, and social events have profound impacts on market movements.

2. Diversify your investment Splurge your assets over different types of investments. This strategy will increase your chances for embedding successful investments and reduce the overall risk.

3. Conduct extensive research Before investing, delve into thorough research about the security or the asset. Look at past trends, read reports and predictions, and make informed decisions.

4. Consider professional help Via financial advisors, or robo-advisors, you can gain professional and tailored advice on managing and growing your wealth.

5. Think long term Successful wealth building often demands long-term strategies over short-term wins. Rome wasn't built in a day, and neither will your wealth.

By understanding and pioneering these profundities of financial markets, one can steeply steer their way to a prosperous life. Remember, the journey to wealthy living starts with sowing seeds of financial consciousness and nurturing them with knowledge and informed decisions.

Chapter 6. Invest to Impress: Strategies for Profitable Investing

Financial investment may appear to be daunting, but with the right strategies and knowledge, it can open doors to abundant prosperity and freedom. This chapter aims to unravel the art of investing, as well as the benefits of a well-thought-out investment strategy. There is no one-size-fits-all approach in the sphere of investing. Hence, it is crucial to understand different strategies, variables, and potentially profitable investments to make sound decisions.

6.1. Understanding Investment Basics

Before diving into the strategies for profitable investing, we have to revisit the basics. Investment, in its simplest form, is the act of allocating resources, often money, with the expectation of generating an income or profit. It typically involves risk of loss and the potential for return. These key elements - risk, return, and the investment itself - are what shapes your investment plans.

Your investment can take on diverse forms - from bond buying to stock purchasing, real estate investing, mutual fund investing, startup funding, to purchasing commodities like gold. Understanding these basics helps in building a foundation upon which solid investment strategies can be crafted.

6.2. The Time Value of Money

The concept of the time value of money is one of the most important principles in finance and investing. The basic idea is that money available at the present is worth more than the same amount in the future due to its potential earning capacity. This financial principle helps investors determine how much money to invest, where, and for how long. Understanding this principle is also crucial in mastering the art of compound interest.

6.3. Investing in Stocks

Stock investing is one of the most popular forms of investing due to the potentially high returns. However, it's important to understand that stocks come with their own set of risks. Thus, you need to employ effective strategies when investing in stocks.

The first and perhaps the most critical element of stock investing is diversification. Investing in a wide array of stocks helps in mitigating risk and providing a safety net for your investment portfolio.

Research is key in stock investing. This means, understanding the company's history, the industry it operates in, its competitors, and its financial statements. Share buying should never be based on a hunch or tip.

Investing in blue-chip stocks, or companies with a history of sound financial performance, is often considered a safe bet. They typically have dependable profits, robust business models, and are often industry leaders.

6.4. Bond Investments

Bonds are considered to be less risky than stocks. They are essentially a loan you make to the issuer in return for interest payments and the principal amount at the end of the term.

Investing in bonds from stable governments and reputable

corporations are considered a safer bet as default chances are quite low. Also, diversifying your bond investments just like your stock investments, further reduces risk.

To enjoy the best of both worlds, consider balanced funds, which combine both bonds and stocks in a balanced ratio. Typically, these funds comprise of 60% stocks and 40% bonds, catering to moderate-risk investors.

6.5. Real Estate and Commodities

Another popular form of investing is in tangible properties such as real estate. Real estate investment is often considered advantageous due to its potential for consistent cash flow, appreciation, and tax advantages.

Investing in commodities like gold, silver, or oil adds another level of diversification to your investment portfolio, providing a cushion against market uncertainties.

6.6. Planning for Retirement

Planning your investments with a long-term perspective helps especially when planning your retirement. Retirement plans like the 401(k) or different types of Individual Retirement Accounts offer specific tax benefits that can help grow your retirement fund.

6.7. Embracing Robo-Advisors

As technology forges forwards, investment methodologies also evolve. Robo-advisors provide a valuable tool that can assist both novice and seasoned investors. They function on algorithms to craft an investment strategy tailored to your risk tolerance and financial goals, making them an excellent tool for your investing arsenal.

While putting these strategies into action, it is vital to remember that all investments come with risks. The age-old advice of not investing more than you can afford to lose still holds true. As you dip your toes into the inviting realm of profitable investing, remember - patience and knowledge are your strongest allies. It's not about timing the market, but about time IN the market.

The strategies mentioned above together create a comprehensive roadmap for profitable investing. Even as you embark on this journey, continue to educate yourself about the dynamic world of investing, and adapt your strategies as necessary. The world of investing offers boundless opportunities. Empowered with the right strategies, you can unlock the doors to abundance and financial freedom.

Chapter 7. Cultivating Prosperity: Smart Savings Techniques

The cornerstone of prosperity rests upon a foundation of diligent savings. However, mere savings aren't enough—what separates the truly prosperous from those rigidly sticking to a middle-class lifestyle is the savvy approach to savings. If you're looking to foster growth in your wealth, read on as we traverse through various ways of evolving beyond basic savings to an ecosystem of mindful and smart savings techniques.

7.1. The Frugal Fortress: Enlist Your Expenses

The first step in your journey to financial abundance starts with understanding where your money flows. It's a detour in your usual spending behavior that requires a meticulous assessment of your expenses. To get a clear picture of your spending habits, list down your everyday costs and segregate them into categories. This way, you get a more detailed breakdown of your expenditure and can identify areas where you might be over-spending.

Living within your means is a mantra for prosperity. There's a sense of empowerment associated with frugality, as knowing where to spend and where to save can help you manage your money more efficiently. By becoming more conscious of your spending habits you can pinpoint areas of unnecessary expense and cut back, saving more in the process.

7.2. A Dose of Preventive Healthcare: Insurance Savings

Health crises can lead to substantial financial stress: an unforeseen medical emergency can derail your financial stability. Health insurance serves as a safety net in such scenarios, so, ensure it isn't overlooked.

Identify an insurance policy that caters to your needs without being burdensomely expensive. Don't hesitate to shop around and compare various insurance policies. The goal is to secure health coverage that offers a balance between comprehensive protection and cost-effectiveness. Also, explore options like Health Savings Accounts (HSAs), which offer the triple-tax advantage—your contributions, interest earnings, and eligible withdrawals are all tax-free.

7.3. Automate Your Savings Journey

The adage "out of sight, out of mind" comes in handy while saving money. Automatic savings ensure that a part of your income is set aside before you even see it, thereby eliminating the temptation to spend it.

Set up with your bank so that with each pay check, money is automatically transferred to a savings account. You could even set up different accounts for various saving goals. This uncomplicated setup requires minimal maintenance and yields significant results over time.

7.4. Investment: The Secret Armory

With the foundation of basic savings, it's time to step towards growth-focused wealth creation—investing. Stocks, bonds, mutual funds, and real estate investments are forms of building wealth that could potentially deliver high returns over time.

While investing requires careful planning and consideration, it's not unachievable. Begin by determining your risk tolerance, investment goals, and time horizon. Focus on a diversified portfolio that will balance potential growth with risk mitigation.

Remember, the goal is to plan your investments properly for a stable financial future, not to chase the latest trends or hot stocks. A cautious, strategic approach to investment is recommended, and if necessary, seek professional advice to guide your investment journey.

7.5. Retirement Planning: A Future-Proof Life

Retirement planning is a crucial aspect of financial health that's often overlooked in the early stages of one's career. However, starting to save for retirement early can ensure a comfortable life in your sunset years.

Consider plans like Individual Retirement Accounts (IRA), 401(k), or employer-sponsored retirement plans, which offer tax benefits. Remember, the sooner you start, the more time your savings have to grow. Even if you can't save a lot initially, starting early provides a cushion of time to take advantage of compound interest, turning your small savings into a substantial fund over the years.

In conclusion, attaining prosperity doesn't happen overnight. It involves careful planning, disciplined saving, prudent expense management, wise investing, and conscious forethought towards retirement. It's about understanding that every penny saved today is a step towards a wealthy tomorrow. So, start at once—evaluate your expenses, secure your health, automate your savings, invest wisely, and don't forget your future self. Your journey to financial freedom awaits!

Chapter 8. Shopping Smarter: Conscious Spending Tactics

Today, the lure of consumerism has countless individuals ensnared in its grip. From the latest tech gadgets that sparkle with novelty to carefully packaged holiday deals that promise unforgettable memories, the sheer scale of spending opportunities might leave you dazed. However, successful wealth management isn't simply about earning more. It's also about spending wisely. Let's delve into the tactful strategies that can ensure your hard-earned money serves you well.

8.1. Considering Needs Vs Wants

Choosing consciously between needs and wants is a foundational step towards smarter shopping. A need refers to those essentials that we genuinely require for survival and a reasonable quality of life. On the other hand, a want represents a desire for something which isn't fundamental to our survival and can be lived without.

Emotional spending often results from an unchecked chase for wants. It's important to articulate the difference between wants and needs and prioritize our expenses accordingly. However, this doesn't mean that wants should always be demonized. Instead, plan your needs first and if you still have room in your budget, only then indulge in fulfilling your wants.

8.2. Creating and Sticking to a Budget

Creating a budget is the cornerstone of conscious spending. To begin with, list out your regular income sources and monthly expenses.

Unmissable bills, groceries, healthcare, insurance, and savings should be your priorities. Deduct these amounts from your monthly income to see how much capital you have for other expenses.

The key is to adhere to your budget. Services like automated bill payments or apps that alert you when you're nearing your spending limit can assist you in this area. Remember, the aim isn't to restrict your enjoyment of life, but to manage your funds effectively.

8.3. Understanding the True Cost of a Purchase

When considering a purchase, it's fundamental to understand its 'whole life cost.' This includes the initial price, maintenance costs, and depreciation value. For example, when buying a car, also factor in the yearly costs of insurance, servicing, fuel consumption, and the loss in value over time. This broader perspective allows you to make informed decisions and shields you from impulse purchases.

8.4. Comparing to Conserve

Before making a purchase, consider different brands, shop around, and find the best value-for-money deal. Sales, discounts, and promos can allow considerable savings, but be cautious not to get enticed into buying things you don't actually need.

8.5. Practicing Mindful Spending

Mindful spending involves being conscious about where your money is going, understanding why you're making a purchase, and recognizing its impact on your financial health. Before making a decision, ask yourself how the expense aligns with your overall money goals and whether it really adds value to your life.

8.6. Buying Quality Products

It might be tempting to buy cheaper products to save money in the short term. However, these products tend to have a shorter lifespan and can lead to more frequent replacements and thus, greater costs in the long run. Investing in quality might require a larger initial outlay but can save you more in the end.

8.7. Avoiding Debt Traps

Taking out loans or using credit cards to finance a lifestyle beyond your means can lead to crippling debt. While these instruments are useful in managing cash flow and emergencies, using them unwisely can result in hefty interest payments that erode your long-term wealth.

In conclusion, shopping smarter doesn't mean stifling your desires or living minimally. Instead, it emphasizes practicing conscious spending habits that enable you to fulfill your needs, treat your wants responsibly, and ultimately, make your money work in your favor. As you implement these tactics, you'll develop a healthy and beneficial relationship with your money, nudging yourself closer to financial prosperity.

Chapter 9. Ready for Rainy Days: An Insight into Emergency Funds

Emergencies transpire unanticipated, yet the financial ramifications they bear can be overwhelming. In the realm of personal finance, an emergency fund serves as a stringently guarded safety net protecting you in times of unexpected fiscal tribulations. It provides a cushion against unfortunate events like job loss, healthcare calamity, car repairs, or any unscheduled expenditure. Cultivating a robust emergency fund is the cornerstone of any sustainable wealth-management strategy, preparing you for the vicissitudes life may adorn.

9.1. Understanding the Emergency Fund

An emergency fund, by definition, is an account for funds accumulated to tackle financial emergencies that are unexpected, instant, and disruptive. A key factor differentiating it from regular savings is its purpose – it isn't for lavish vacations or buying your dream car, but for being steadfast in economically strenuous times.

To calculate how robust your fund should be, consider your lifestyle, monthly costs, financial responsibilities and risk tolerance. Typically, experts recommend having three to six months' worth of living expenses set aside in your emergency fund. This estimate offers a reasonable buffer during life's unpredicted setbacks without creating undue strain on daily budgeting.

Remember an emergency fund is not a luxury, but a necessity. An optimal fund size can eclipse financial stress, empowering you to make stronger decisions not based on immediate scarcity but on long-term financial health.

9.2. Building Your Emergency Fund

Initiating your emergency fund might appear daunting, particularly if you're already wrestling with outstanding debts or precarious income. However, with a strategic financial plan and disciplined approach, you can construct an emergency nest egg that's capable of cushioning hardships. Here's how:

1. Evaluate your expenses: The first step is to scrutinize your monthly expenses. Keep track of every penny spent, categorize them and identify any potential savings.

2. Establish a goal: Once you apprehend your monthly expenditure, determine your ideal emergency fund size, generally equivalent to six months' worth of expenses.

3. Devise a budget: Draft a budget, spotlighting areas where you can economize without compromising on necessities. The surplus funds saved should be directed toward your emergency fund.

4. Regular Savings: Allocate a certain percentage of your income to go directly into your emergency fund. Automatic deductions can assist in cultivating a habit of regular savings.

5. Snowball method: If you have debts, consider using the snowball method. Once a smaller debt is paid off, apply that payment to the next larger debt, gradually building momentum and freeing up income.

Building an emergency fund isn't a sprint but a marathon. It may take some time to achieve your desired goal, but remember, any contribution, however small, paves the way to greater financial stability.

9.3. Making the Best Use of your Fund

It's essential to determine when to use your emergency fund. These funds are specifically constructed for unforeseen and necessary expenses, like medical emergencies or sudden job loss. Avoid tapping into these funds for planned expenditures or wants.

Furthermore, your emergency fund must be easily accessible. Keeping these funds in high-yield savings accounts or money market accounts ensures it remains liquid, yet continues to grow modestly over time.

One popular strategy involves dividing your fund across different banking products. For instance, keeping one month's worth of expenses in a checking account for immediate accessibility, three months' worth in a savings account for semi-liquid safety, and the remaining in high-yield bonds or certificates of deposits for earning interest while maintaining security.

9.4. Grow your Emergency Fund: A Final Word

Growing your emergency fund doesn't mean endlessly saving; it involves balancing between saving, investing, and living. Including your fund in your regular budgeting, monitoring expenses, and leveraging windfall gains for fund contribution are some of the successful strategies to consider.

Remember, the objective of the emergency fund is financial security. It supports you during crises, ensuring you don't fall into debt traps or compromise your living standards. It's the umbrella ready for your financial rainy days, safeguarding your wealth tree from harsh winds of unexpected difficulties while nurturing the roots of your wealthy living.

Chapter 10. Planning for a Worry-Free Future: Retirement Strategies

Discovering the concept of retirement can be a defining moment in a person's life, simultaneously producing feelings of excitement and apprehension. Retirement doesn't have to be a time of fear and financial uncertainty. By pouring your effort into well thought-out strategies now, you can secure a worry-free and comfortable future. The cornerstones of such strategies are understanding your current financial situation, determining your retirement goals, creating a sustainable saving and investment plan, and incorporating the right insurance policies.

10.1. Understanding Your Financial Situation

Having a profound understanding of your current financial situation is an essential first step in planning for a stress-free retirement. It requires creating a comprehensive list of your income sources, assets, and liabilities. Income sources refer to your consistent streams of earnings, possibly from a regular job, business, part-time gig, or passive income sources. Assets include everything you own, such as your house, car, bank savings, stocks, or retirement accounts. Liabilities, on the other hand, refer to your debts or financial obligations—be it a home mortgage, car loan, credit card bills, etc.

After listing all these down, subtract your liabilities from the sum of your income sources and assets to approximate your net worth. This exercise illuminates where you stand financially and sets the roots for future planning.

10.2. Determining Retirement Goals

Your retirement goals should align with the lifestyle you envision for yourself during your sunset years. Consider questions like: At what age do you see yourself retiring? Do you plan to maintain your current lifestyle, or do you wish to downsize or even upgrade it? Do you envision yourself traveling often or perhaps pursuing an expensive hobby? Do you see yourself living in your home country or settling in another part of the globe?

Each answer will have implications on your savings and investment plans and thus, should be thought through clearly. Once your goals are clear, you can estimate your required retirement funds—this is the number you'll aim for in your saving and investment plan.

10.3. Creating a Saving and Investment Plan

A saving and investment plan serves as a roadmap to take you from your current financial situation to your retirement goal. The key to success is to starting early, being consistent, and observing patience.

Initially, allocate some part of your income towards an emergency fund equivalent to three to six months of your living expenses. This fund will serve as a pad for unforeseen circumstances while you're still working or even in retirement.

For your retirement savings, consider opening a specific retirement savings account. Depending on your location, there are often tax advantages to saving in such accounts, aside from the fact that the money is automatically set aside for your golden years.

Meanwhile, investments can significantly help speed up your wealth accumulation. Consider an appropriate mix of bonds, traditional stocks, mutual funds, and real estate, depending on your risk appetite, age, and the current economic situation.

Remember to revisit and adjust your savings and investment plan over time, adapting to income changes, windfalls, financial emergencies, life events (like marriage or children), and fluctuations in the market.

10.4. Insurance Coverage in Retirement

Finally, for a worry-free future, it is paramount to protect yourself from health-related financial shocks that often accompany aging. Thus, having appropriate health insurance coverage is a non-negotiable part of your retirement plan. Based on your current health, family history, and personal lifestyle, project the kind of coverage you think you'll need in the future, and start planning for it from now. Health insurance and long-term care insurance should be part of your plan.

Annuity policies can also ensure a steady stream of income in your retirement years, providing additional peace of mind. However, approach annuity with proper understanding and caution because it is a long-term commitment and may come with substantial fees.

Remember, your retirement journey doesn't have to feel like walking a tightrope across an abyss. The steps outlined above—understanding your financial situation, setting precise retirement goals, formulating a formidable savings and investment plan, and incorporating the right insurance policies—can transform the maze of retirement planning into a well-lit path. Craft your plan strategically and review it periodically to ensure you are on the right track towards a golden, worry-free future.

Chapter 11. Your Wealth, Your Legacy: Estate Planning Essentials

Financial planning can feel like a labyrinth at times, but a significant portion of it requires particularly keen attention, and that is – Estate Planning. It is quintessentially a forward-thinking process that shapes how your affluence and legacy will continue, even when you're not around.

11.1. The Basics of Estate Planning

In essence, estate planning is the process through which an individual specifies how their wealth will be allocated or managed upon incapacitation or death. Assets can entail anything from physical goods (real estate, cars, jewelry) to intangible ones (investments, life insurance, retirement funds).

This process mainly seeks to achieve these primary objectives: . Protecting the wealth you have amassed over your lifetime . Ensuring your assets are distributed as per your wishes . Guarding your heirs from cumbersome taxes and legal extents . Appointing custodians for underage beneficiaries

In order to facilitate these objectives smooth as silk, there are various estate planning tools that can be utilized, which include wills, trusts, power of attorney, health care surrogate, and more.

11.2. Wills and Trusts in Estate Planning

The two most prominent instruments in estate planning are wills and trusts.

A will is a legal document that outlines your wishes pertaining to the distribution of your assets and the care of any minor children. It comes into effect after death. Having a well-constructed will is paramount to prevent potential disputes amongst beneficiaries.

Trusts, on the other hand, are legal entities you create to hold and regulate your assets. Trusts are advantageous in bypassing the typically lengthy and expensive probate process that follows death. Trusts can also be designed to provide for a beneficiary who may not be well-equipped to manage the property on their own.

11.3. Estate Taxes and Legalities

A substantial part of estate planning involves tax planning. An understanding of the estate federal taxes, as well as state inheritance and estate taxes, can help you lay a strategy to limit the tax liabilities. Bear in mind that estate tax laws are subject to change; hence, keeping updated is crucial.

Another critical aspect of estate planning is immersing yourself in the legalities. Everything from defining your beneficiaries clearly, updating your estate plan in response to life changes, or law changes, can all contribute to an efficient estate plan.

11.4. Estate planning and Retirement Funds

One common misconception regarding retirement benefits like 401(k)s or IRAs is the belief that they're protected from estate taxes. On the contrary, these may be subject to both estate and income taxes. However, other pivotal benefits such as naming a beneficiary for these assets can bypass the probate process. An estate planning professional can guide you best in streamlining your retirement benefits into your overall estate planning.

11.5. Choosing the Correct Executor and Legal Counsel

Choosing an executor (or trustee, in the case of a living trust) who'll carry out your wishes as per your estate plan is crucial. This can be an individual like a family member, or an entity like a bank or a legal professional. Your legal counsel can assist you with this decision and ensure the estate planning process aligns with your wishes and legal requirements.

11.6. All About Updating Your Estate Plan

Simply having an estate plan isn't enough. Life changes, and with it, your needs and wishes. Therefore, your estate plan should reflect these changes. Be it marriage, a newborn, divorce, or death of a loved one; all major changes necessitate an update in your estate plan.

Estate planning is an ongoing process that evolves with your life, so regular reviews are advisable. By keeping your plan updated, you're ensuring that you leave behind an orderly estate, well-protected heirs, and airtight financial security that echoes your life's relentless pursuit of prosperity.

11.7. Concluding Thoughts

Embarking on the estate planning journey could seem imposing, especially given its long-term implications. However, with professional guidance and strategic planning, you can ensure your legacy lives on according to your intentions. If you take the time now to make effective financial decisions, it can guarantee the security of your hard-earned wealth and offer a layer of protection to your loved ones when they most need it.

After all, estate planning isn't just about passing down wealth; it's also about passing down your values, your life's work, and your passion. Therefore, take these steps today to ensure your wealth continues to foster prosperity for you and your loved ones. Remember, your wealth should live as long as your legacy does, and effective estate planning is the golden key to that treasure.